Musings For Madie

Stephanie Malbasa

Dedication

Dedicated to Madeline Christine Malbasa

With Love,

Baba

Like mile markers on a map, memories connect me to my past and guide me to the future.

Dear Reader,

Writing this journal of quotes and my reflections for my granddaughter was a very personal sharing of my thoughts and feelings. Whether we agree or disagree with others, it is my firm belief that we need to read and listen to each other. And then we need to examine that information for ourselves and know ourselves. I believe that she and her young peers are our hope for a wonderful future. Sharing my thoughts with her and now with you, I hope you realize that life gives us life. There will be good days and bad days. It is how we face each moment that counts.

Sincere thanks are owed to Katherine Essig, Deborah Zupkovich and Ann Marie Holtz for their careful reading, editing and encouragement. I would like to also thank the staff at Writer's Critique. And most of all, I thank Stephen Malbasa for encouraging me to share this writing with you and for sharing our adventures together.

Thank you, dear reader and thinker. We are all a work in progress and our work is not yet finished. There is much to be done. Be who you want to be!

With kind regards,

Stephanie

A Psalm of Life

Tell me not, in mournful numbers,
Life is but an empty dream!
For the soul is dead that slumbers,
And things are not what they seem.

Life is real! Life is earnest!
And the grave is not its goal;
Dust thou art, to dust returnest,
Was not spoken of the soul.

Not enjoyment and not sorrow,
Is our destined end or way;
But to act, that each tomorrow
Find us farther than today.

Art is long, and Time is fleeting,
And our hearts, though stout and brave,
Still, like muffled drums are beating
Funeral marches to the grave.

In the world's broad field of battle,
In the bivouac of Life.
Be not like dumb, driven cattle!
Be a hero in the strife!

Trust no future; however pleasant!
Let the dead Past bury its dead!
Act-act in the living Present!
Heart within, and God o'erhead!

Lives of great men all remind us
We can make our lives sublime,
And, departing leave behind us
Footprints on the sands of time.

Footprints, that perhaps another,
Sailing o'er life's solemn main,
A forlorn and shipwrecked brother,
Seeing, shall take heart again.

Let us then, be up and doing,
With a heart for any fate;
Still achieving, still pursuing
Learn to labor, and learn to wait.

Henry Wadsworth Longfellow

"The aim of life is to live, and to live means to be aware, joyously, drunkenly, serenely, divinely aware."

Henry Miller

What a gift to live life-aware!
It is so easy to get bogged down with 'to do
lists' and getting things done that it is easy to be unaware. What a
delight to truly be present
in what I am doing, to be joyous with the
people in my life.

"You must take action now that move you towards your goals.
Develop a sense of urgency in your life."

H. Jackson Brown

The lyrics from the musical <u>Hamilton</u> – "Why do you write like you're running out of time," conveyed Hamilton's sense of urgency. Indeed, not just thinking about what I want to do but taking action.

Aspirations, dreams, and goals are wonderfully important, but to **act upon them** is how those dreams and goals become reality.

To do so with a sense of urgency keeps us focused. That idea 'if not now, when? If not me, then who?'

"Unless someone like you cares a whole awful lot, nothing is going to get better. It's not."

Dr. Seuss

How many times I've found that the children's books of Dr. Seuss have had such profound wisdom. I believe each of us has a "calling."

While I believe it comes from God, others may just feel that human beings are here on earth for a reason. In either case, I think we need to listen to our inner selves, for that voice that calls to our hearts and causes us to feel and to care deeply and passionately.

"God gave you a gift of 86,400 seconds today. Have you used one to say 'thank you'?"

William Arthur Ward

Years ago, I began writing a list of prayers and gratitudes. I call it my "Golden List" – probably not original – more likely inspired by an inspirational movie I watched. The list has changed my life. To pray for and give thanks for those I love and for those I find difficult to love, brings me great joy each morning. I will write more on my Golden List later, but one of my first "thank yous" is for you and for the people in my life.

"Quality is not an act; it is a habit."

Aristotle

It takes time and attention to perform or create a quality performance or product. Making corrections may take more time than doing it right the first time.

As children we learn to brush our teeth, to say 'please' and 'thank you', and these become habits. Habits can be good or bad. It's important from time to time to reflect on our personal habits. A few years ago, I developed the valley girl habit of adding the word 'like' to every sentence, and I also developed the habit of thinking if I waited until the last minute to start a project, the adrenaline would kick in and help me get the work done more quickly. More quickly -yes; more accurately -no. {Well, *like* it is *like* really hard to break some habits!}

"Life ceases for the rest of us just when we are getting ready for it…It is not that we have a short time to live, but that we waste a lot of it."

Seneca wrote to his friend Paulinus

We need to get up, dress up, and show up. That's probably someone's quote too. However, I'd like to expound a bit. Getting up after a good night's sleep and not wasting time in those early morning hours can really set the tone for the rest of the day. So, take those first few moments to pray and stretch your mind and body.

Then, live your day.

"Imagination was given to man to compensate him for what he is not; a sense of humor to console him for what he is."

Francis Bacon

Imagination is truly a great gift. It allows us to envision a better world, our better selves.

Sometimes, we imagine negative things, and that's okay too. It helps us to be aware, to take caution.

One of the greatest gifts is the ability to laugh, to find joy. To laugh at ourselves is perhaps one of the greatest gifts we may have. It keeps us humble; it keeps us real.

I like to think my imagination helps me be my better self and my sense of humor lets me accept myself as I am right now.

"Wherever you are – be all there."

Jim Elliot

When you are late for even your best friends, you send a message that you are more important than them. No one cares how busy you may be or what caused you to be late. As a young working mother, I refused breakfast or dinner meetings or drinks after work because I knew that my priority was to have my children ready for school in the morning and to have dinner with my family in the evening. For some, career responsibility may not afford the luxury of opting out of such events, and extra care may be needed to ensure all aspects of one's nonwork life -taking care of one's body, mind, and soul- are addressed.

Firm handshakes, eye contact, and active listening convey to the other person that he or she is important. Never be so arrogant that you feel like you don't have to listen (and hear) what someone else is saying.

"Take care of your body. It's the only place you have to live."

Jim Rohn

It sounds so simple, doesn't it? But I can attest that is one concept I wished I learned much earlier in life. I was born with good genes, for the most part. But I also thought I'd always be slim and healthy and strong. That's basically not true for any of us. If we overeat or overindulge in anything, most of all food and drink, eventually we will gain weight. If we don't exercise, our muscles atrophy. We will not only look overweight; we will lose whatever strength we gained in our youth. Sound depressing? It is!!

One doctor years ago cautioned about not staying strong by saying, "You don't want to be one of those old ladies who can't get up off the toilet!" – okay, way too visual, but I think you understand my point.

Only you can take care of you! It's important not only for you but for all those you love. Take care of you!

"The more I wonder, the more I love."

Alice Walker

What a gift to be curious! Abraham Joshua Herschel wrote that "wonder rather than doubt is the root of all knowledge." I've always admired and been in awe of children who constantly ask, "Why?" Your Dad, Madie, has always been that person – The one who asked "Why" to the point of sometimes driving me crazy. But his curiosity caused me to learn more, to appreciate that I didn't have all the answers.

Wonder embodies more than just getting an answer. It also involves understanding and appreciation. Wonder is a journey for the mind and spirit to truly explore who we are, who we want to love, and who we want to be. Curiosity impels us to be as tenacious as a child and as daring to explore and to try with wonder, rather than doubt, what lies ahead of us.

The love of others and of ourselves is a gift.

"Your destiny is to fulfill those things upon which you focus more intently. So, choose to keep your focus on that which is truly magnificent, beautiful, uplifting and joyful. Your life is always moving toward something."

Ralph Marston

It really is amazing when I focus on what is uplifting and how those tasks or people that make me weary or sad are put into perspective. When I focus on what is magnificent, it causes me to get excited about whatever it is I am doing. I hope you always are able to find joy in what you choose to do and with the people with whom you spend time.

As for destiny, I think it is in large part determined by what we think, what we dream, how we act and what we do. I am determined to forge my destiny to be magnificent and I pray for your destiny to be as well!

"We have to leave the wilderness of your intuition. What you'll discover will be wonderful. What you'll discover is yourself."

Alan Alda

I don't know how you feel about your intuition, but I have long been attached to and am dependent on my intuition. It's my sense of feeling that I already know a person's character or even what's going to happen. I've always considered it one of my gifts. Not as strong as ESP, but definitely a strong Irish "fey" or knowing.

But it is steeped in a wilderness of preconceived notions that could possibly be wrong. By letting go of or challenging my intuition, I have learned that some ideas are based on historical prejudices that family or friends shared, and I merely just agreed and did not question. Superstitions, fears and worry cannot exist if I leave the wilderness of my intuition and explore the wonderful world. In the process, I discover myself.

"Men must live and create. Live to the point of tears."

Albert Camus

"Live to the point of tears" – Tears of joy, tears of sadness but even the tears of sadness come because of the joy that preceded. I think of the loss of loved ones – my grandfather, my sister, my Mom, my Dad and so many others. I cried because I loved them and had happy memories.

I have wept over injustices and loss. Yet, those tears that welled up released my emotions and reminded me that to live is to care.

I cry at movies, I cry when I hear beautiful music, and I cry at every children's concert, although I try to just smile.

Living to the point of tears embodies living and connecting with others.

As for the part 'live and create' – how we choose to create our lives is our life. What we do, what we do for others, whom we care about and for whom we care – that is life, living to the point of tears.

"The capacity of delight is the gift of paying attention."

Julia Margaret Cameron

Tara Branch wrote, "[Paying] Attention is the most basic form of love. By paying attention, we let ourselves be touched by life, and our hearts naturally become more open and engaged."

Attention is a little different from focus in my opinion. I get very focused on my tasks, my thoughts, and my ideas. I think attention is being aware of that which is other than ourselves. It is seeing a person and looking and smiling at them and possibly making their day a bit brighter. It is being aware of someone else's feelings or needs.

"Attention!" It is a call to sit up, listen and take notice.

"I want to be used up when I die, for the harder I work, the more I live. I rejoice in life for its own sake."

"George Bernard Shaw"

There are only so many days any of us have to live. It's always amused me to help clients with their wills to say, "if you die..." as if any of us are not going to die.

I think each of us has talents and gifts to use in this life; we have a purpose; we are supposed to use those gifts and talents - That is our life's work.

It is while in the process of using my talents and gifts and working to do what I feel I am called to do that I find I am able to live life to the fullest.

Life is sometimes hard, but like Shaw, I want to rejoice in life for its own sake.

"Very little is needed to make a happy life; it is all within yourself, in your way of thinking."

Marcus Aurelius

In school, we started each morning with the "Pledge of Allegiance." When I went to parochial school, we went to Mass before we walked over to our classrooms. Recent journal reports say that teachers are asking students 'how they feel' in the morning before classes begin. Reflecting on the different starts to my mornings and those of students today, I cherish mine.

Sitting in that church, I had time to quiet myself, to get over the spats with my siblings, my mother's criticism, the school bus stop and ride and to just meditate (even though I didn't know what that was back then). Standing in school for the Pledge of Allegiance instilled a strong message: that I am a citizen and I can stand up for what our country believes in and strives to attain.

Instead of asking students how they feel, perhaps we need to help them engage, to think of others, to just start doing the work of the day; and in the process help them learn that 'happiness is a choice.'

"The highest reward for a person's toil is not what they get for it, but what they become by it."

John Raskin

Sometimes, I admit, I get discouraged. People say I don't charge enough for the work that I do, although some people for whom I work think (or make me feel) that I charge too much. I really liked this quote because I started to understand that I, as a person, have evolved. I probably have enough stories to write an eleven-season series – 'The client secrets I'll take to my grave.'

But seriously, the true value of the work one does is how it affects them and molds them, hopefully, to be a better person.

I learn so much from the people I have met in my life through my work. They've had a profound influence. I hope and pray that your work leads you to meet wonderful, inspiring and quality people that reward you not only financially, but also enrich you as a human being.

"To such an extent does nature delight and abound in variety that among her trees there is not one plant to be found that is exactly like another; and not only among the plants but among the boughs, the leaves, the fruits, you will not find one which is exactly similar to another."

Leonardo da Vinci

Each of us is unique. Isn't that amazing?
It's okay that I am different.
It's natural!

Embrace your uniqueness!

"Words are more than what is set down on paper. It takes the human voice to infuse them with deeper meaning."

Maya Angelou

I love <u>your</u> voice! Keep using it to debate, to talk, to sing!

When I listen to a song or a poem read aloud, it takes on a whole new meaning. Perhaps the human voice conveys not just a message but also expresses the emotion of the speaker and then evokes feelings in me.

I truly believe the beauty of art or music is its capacity to not only convey the message of what the artist is trying to say, but also feelings. It is feelings that make us truly human; the ability to convey not just facts but how we feel is what sets us apart and reveals our humanity.

"If you listen to your fears, you will die never knowing what a great person you might have been."

Robert H. Schuller

You are fearless! Sometimes in life we talk ourselves into thinking we can't do something, or we're not good enough, or we might not succeed, or any number of negative thoughts.

Rereading this quote reminded me that I must not listen to my fears. Sometimes, the tasks of life are huge and it seems that I will never finish. It's a fear that sometimes stops me in my tracks.

Always try to do your best. Meet people and connect with them. Ask questions. Demand answers, not only from others, but from yourself.

Remain fearless!

"The soul should always stand ajar, ready to welcome the ecstatic experience."

Emily Dickinson

Being open to new adventures, meeting new friends, walking a different path, reading a different genre, listening to different music, all enrich our lives.

A little boy was flying his kite and it crashed. I was able to help him get it back in the air. His sheer delight and his hand reaching out in thanks warmed my soul.

Life is full of every day miracles to enjoy if we keep our souls open.

"Clear thinking requires courage rather than intelligence."

Thomas Szasy

One can be smart and learn all kinds of information. But, I believe clear thinking really does take courage, the courage to say, "Wait, I disagree" knowing that our opinion may be ridiculed or even reviled.

It's so easy to go along with other people's ideas and ways of thinking. Growing up in a small town without much exposure to the whole world, it was, or seemed, natural to believe what everyone else said about people who were different. However, my Dad would say, there are a lot of peculiar people in the world, but they don't seem so strange once you know their names.

I am reminded of the story of the young woman who asked her mother why she always cut off the ends of the roast. The mother called her mother, who called the great-grandmother. Great Grandma laughed and said it was because she didn't have a roaster big enough.

Question! Challenge what you think you know!

"Take care of your body. It's the only place you have to live."

Jim Rohn

[yes, again]

If I could revise my younger self, I would implore myself to exercise every day, stay strong and eat as healthy and sensibly as possible. A woman's body goes through many changes as we age. It was easy to think - 'I'll be fine, I'll be okay, I'll stay slim, I'll defy my genetics, my predispositions and my unhealthy habits' – NOT TRUE! My family was filled with relatives who drank too much, smoked and ate to excess. I did learn that I did not want to be like them.

So many of my friends are having knee and hip replacements and fighting cancers. I feel so blessed at the moment. However, life gives us life and who knows how I will be in the years to come; however, I'm going to continue to try to be strong, flexible and have the best body I can have for the rest of my life.

"First say to yourself what would you be and then do what you have to do."

Epectetus

It sounds so simple. In truth, it really is. So many people don't stop and think about "what would you be?" I'm a believer in vocation. For me, I feel that there is an inner voice in each of us. Some would say it is God or the Holy Spirit calling us to be what we are meant to be. Ideas, inspirations, and thoughts come from that inner voice. Some people channel this by meditation, prayer, being still, or just letting go of all the distractions for a few moments each day. It's really quite amazing!

And then act. It's not going to be easy. It's the work of life.

And play. If you listen to that inner voice, you will be called to do both.

"A healthy attitude is contagious, but don't wait to catch it from others. Be a carrier."

Tom Stoppard

Just as I believe love is a choice and happiness is a choice, I think having and keeping a healthy attitude is a choice. But what is a healthy attitude? It's more than being optimistic. It's stronger than hoping all will be okay. A healthy attitude exudes confidence and poise. Perhaps it is in having humility that one is grounded; one is real.

There are things in life we cannot change. I stopped growing in sixth grade, limiting my opportunities to be a basketball player or a supermodel. Well, those might not have been my aspirations, but if they were, I would have to change my attitude from being depressed or angry to an attitude of adventure and curiosity about what I might be able to accomplish.

Always have a fearless attitude.

"No matter how you feel, get up, dress up and show up."

Regina Brett

Seneca wrote to his friend Paulinus, "Life ceases for the rest of us just when we are getting ready for it… it is not that we have a short time to live, but that we waste a lot of it.

As a teenager, I would stay up too late, drinking coffee with my Dad at 11 p.m., then finally going to bed at 2 a.m., and then getting up a 6:30 a.m. to catch the 7 a.m. bus. Admittedly, back then, dressing up took precedence over reading (I don't think glancing at the headlines and listening to the radio count), and exercise consisted of running up and down the stairs to assemble what was needed for the day.

We do need to get up, dress up and show up!

Getting up after a good night's sleep and not wasting time in those early morning hours really can set a tone for the rest of the day. Taking those first few moments to pray, to stretch mind and body.

"When you arise in the morning, think what a precious privilege it is to be alive – to breathe, to think, to enjoy, to love."

Marcus Aurelius

When I talk about 'dressing up,' I am referring to the need to consider what you are saying about yourself and to the people you may meet by your choice of style or mode of dress. I don't mean high fashion or the latest trends, although I still admire a man that looks good in a suit, tie and crisp shirt and I appreciate a lovely dress and smart shoes on a lady. Basically, be clean and neat, hands and face clean, nails and hair groomed.

Then show up.

It is such a privilege to be alive. I hope to act like I am thankful for this privilege each day.

"Let us always meet each other with a smile, for the smile is the beginning of love."

Mother Teresa

My Mom used to say, "Smile and say hello. You might be the only person that smiles at that person today."

Sage advice. And it has always been my philosophy.

As a teenager, there was a couple who were gymnasts that came and did an assembly in the gym. The fellow chatted nonstop as he did his part of the routine. Meanwhile, the young woman would cartwheel and handspring across the mat and land in front of the group and with a wide, bright smile just say "Hi!!" She was so very endearing that I never forgot the fun and laughter that she brought that day.

Whose day can you brighten?

"Do you wish to rise? Begin by descending. You plan a tower that will pierce to the clouds? Lay first the foundation of humility."

Saint Augustine

There is a country music song, "Always be humble and kind," by Tim McGraw. 'Humble', 'humility' were words that I did not quite grasp. I misunderstood 'humble' to mean simple or poor, as 'he was a simple, humble man' – as in not very motivated. I was wrong!

Humility embodies being real. To know who you are at your very core is the building block. Humility is not caring what others think, not putting on airs that we are other than whom we are.

I'm always offended by the name-droppers who feel they need to tell me about important people they know. Instead, tell me about what is real – who really matters to you, what is really important to you. Actually, let me examine for myself who is important to me, what is important, what makes me real, what makes me human.

"Life is a balancing act. You have multiple roles and goals, and you can do it all – just not all at once."

Denise Morrison

So true! Many years ago, I attended an event where Leslie Stahl was the featured speaker. She spoke about being a professional woman, a reporter, a celebrity, and her personal life. She gave a wonderful analogy that the roles we as human beings try to balance are like balls that we are trying to juggle. "We just need to remember which ones are glass!"

We try to do good things – take care of ourselves, learn, help others, work, volunteer. However, that doesn't mean the choice to do one thing over another is good vs. evil. They are choices we make.

Essentially, for me, I pray and hope that God helps me know which balls are glass – to focus on what's most important.

"We think too much and feel too little."

Charlie Chaplin

In 1940, Charlie Chaplin made a film called "The Great Dictator" where he plays the dictator, Hinkle (aka Hitler) and ghetto Jewish barber. At the time of the film, the US was not at war with Germany. Chaplin masterfully, through humor and satire, revealed what was happening under Hitler and Mussolini. As I watched the film, I thought I needed to think less, learn more, do more, and feel more.

We are driven by what we care about. I want to always care about what is important and then care enough to do something about it!

"I shall allow no man to belittle my soul by making me hate him."

Booker T. Washington

There have been times when I have met a person who makes me feel angry by either hurting me or someone I love. There is, for me, a fine line between anger and rage. What we do with our anger can be a huge challenge. Revenge? It is not sweet. But speaking up against injustice is imperative.

There is a line in the musical <u>Oklahoma</u> –"I don't say I'm no better than anybody else, but I'll be damned if I ain't just as good."

As people hurt you in life (and I hope and pray they won't) try to remember two important lessons: The first is don't give the other person the power to judge who you are. That power only belongs to you and God. The second is "don't lower yourself to their level "(my Dad would say). Just because mean things are said to you, doesn't mean you should be mean as well. Don't belittle your soul!

"There is no pain so great as the memory of joy in present grief."

Aeschylus

Loss. We were so close, we'd come so far, we were such a team, and now it's over. The memory of joys. Death. I loved him so very much, and now he is gone. I can still see in my mind's eye...I can still feel... I can still hear...

And the pain of those memories of joy still brings tears to my eyes and heart.

"If you laugh, you think, and you cry, that's a full day. That's a heck of a day! You do that seven days a week, you're going to be something special."

Jim Valvano

"The world is a book, and those who do not travel read only a page."

Saint Augustine

Be a traveler, not a tourist? A tourist sees the sights, but a traveler is where one's feet are – aware of people, the sights, the sounds, the smells, the culture, the feelings.

Many years ago, my school teacher friend brought her class from Pierpont to Cleveland. Most of the third graders were children of farmers. Coming to the city was a big deal. They went on the Good Time cruise ship, saw the rapid trains coming into the Terminal Tower, a TV station and went up and down escalators – the highlight? Going through a revolving door. It has always reminded me that sometimes I need to travel in my own neighborhood and appreciate all it has to offer.

Having lived in Switzerland during my junior year of college and exploring neighboring countries taught me so very much, not only about where I traveled but about myself.

Happy trails to you!

"Worry never robs tomorrow of its sorrow, it only saps today of its joy."

Leo Buscaglia

Often, we worry for nothing. Usually, what I worry about doesn't happen. For me, the anxiety that builds when I worry causes me to not be present in the now. My worrying is not going to make something happen or not happen.

Life gives us life. Worry is just one way to try to control the future. But, if I worry that the wind will blow a tree over and I will be without power, it is not my worry that controls the wind. It is a waste of time. Embrace each day and what is to come.

"When will we realize that the unfolding process of our lives is so much richer and varied then we ever could have planned? The unplanned and uncontrolled gifts we receive add color to the tapestry of living."

Anne Wilson Schaef

Go with the flow, ride the wave, and stop trying to control everything in life.

"When we were children, we used to think that when we were grown up we would no longer be vulnerable. But to grow up is to accept vulnerability…To be alive is to be vulnerable."

Madeleine L. Engle

If I think of all the experiences that have shaped my life and been most impactful, I find my vulnerability ever present. We give ourselves to the universe by what we say and do. Sometimes our thoughts and actions are accepted, and sometimes they are not. But we speak and act. It is what shapes are compassion, character, integrity, gratitude and fortitude.

To be vulnerable is to be ourselves in the universe and to be open to be received, to be understood, and to be loved.

"You are only afraid if you are not in harmony with yourself.
People are afraid because they have never owned up to
themselves."

Hemann Hess

I read once that fear and self-abuse go together. All of us are afraid sometimes. I fear that my clients will be angry if I don't get work done on time or if I make mistakes. Yet, it is important that I am truthful and admit what I know and don't know.

Fear can cause us to be compulsive workaholics by making ourselves indispensable. But to whom? I want to be passionate about my work but also passionate about my play and about the time for myself.

To be able to make choices for ourselves, we need to take into account our fears. When we face our fears, we gain courage.

Sometimes, it takes courage to play or even take a nap.

"The value of life is not in its duration, but in donation. You are not important because of how long you live; you are important because of how effective you live."

Myles Monroe

Giving of one's time, treasures, and talents is what everyone wants. Board members are asked to give, get, or get off.

The first part of this quote is so very true. The second part, though is food for thought. There's an old Chinese saying: 'Don't give away all your stuff.' Sometimes, we can be so busy trying to please everybody else that we burn ourselves out. Or we spend so much time giving to something that maybe we neglect the people closest to us.

Sometimes, we need to give to ourselves through rest, relaxation, or just a long walk.

"Today is life - The only life you are sure of. Make the most of today. Get interested in something. Shake yourself awake. Develop a hobby. Let the winds of enthusiasm sweep through you. Live today with gusto."

Dale Carnegie

When Geda was a teenager at 13 or 14, he got the name "Big" because of his height. His brother, "Bopper" gave him a baseball mitt that he inscribed with "Think Big!" And that's what Geda does; he thinks big. Years ago, when it came time to name our first boat, he wanted to name it 'Think Big'; but we agreed on the word "Aspire" and we started the charity, 'Aspire II Nav Foundation' to help others aspire to navigate the challenges of life.

Being interested, being fully present and aspiring to live each and every day with gusto makes each and every day wonderful.

"I am always doing that which I cannot do, in order that I may learn how to do it."

Pablo Picasso

I like to read about artists and writers and view their work. Their zeal to understand and share their insights with the rest of us inspires me.

This quote was jotted down the same day my Bible verse of the day was from Proverbs 1:7 "To have knowledge, you must first have reverence for the Lord. Stupid people have no respect for wisdom and refuse to learn."

The ability and desire to learn is a gift. We learn by doing, by experiencing and being attentive to others.

May you always have a desire to learn!

"It's none of their business that you have to learn to write. Let them think you were born that way."

Ernest Hemingway

He sounds just like my Mother: "It's nobody's business". Okay, not always great advice from my mother, but to a certain extent, there is wisdom in not bothering yourself with what other people think.

Do what you love! We are always learning our craft. I'm not talking about arrogance and boastfulness, but rather, to keep learning and honing our skills so it looks to the outside world as if what we are doing is easy.

"Don't be afraid to give up the good to go for the great."

John D. Rockefeller

I think you understand this one from listening to your senior speech about quitting.

Sometimes, it's easy for me to get bogged down in doing good or continuing to do what I know I do well. My personal example is as a young attorney, I was a good generalist taking on small cases; but it was not going to be sustainable physically, emotionally, or financially. I needed to do something more specialized so I could be with my sons and set my own hours. So, I developed a focus on estate planning.

Today, I am re-examining what is "great" for the future. What do I want to learn? How physically fit can I be? What am I going to consider doing that will leave the world better for me having lived?

*"Just don't give up trying to do what you really want to do.
Where there is love and inspiration, I don't think you can go
wrong."*

Ella Fitzgerald

I am reminded of Rosie. She and Butch (Aunt Alice's Mom and Dad) had a son, Gene, who was my older sister's age, born in the late 1940s. He had a condition that I think was muscular dystrophy. Doctors told Rosie her son would never walk and would be mentally challenged. Rosie found therapists in Cleveland, a three-hour trip away from home, and drove him 3 times a week so that he could learn to crawl, walk, write and read. Rosie's tenacity and love inspired her to find ways to help her son and defy the doctors' predictions in every way.

Choosing what you really want to do may not at first seem apparent. But, I believe if we listen and pray, the answers do come.

"Be bold and mighty forces will come to your aid."

Goethe

That's what faith embodies. It never ceases to amaze me when I am bold how things seem to just work out. Sometimes, it may seem silly like believing I will find a parking space right in front of my destination because I believe it will be there. To be bold, one must know their strengths and weaknesses. Being bold is not about being rash; it is about being confident that you can do it. I think I felt bold when I started to give a speech. At the start, it's stepping out in front of people, overcoming fear and then feeling the mighty force of people reacting; understanding my message.

Sometimes, I've felt strength or a second wind; at other times, a gentle calm as my nervousness or anxiety threaten to stop me.

May you be bold and always have mighty forces come your way.

"Life is the art of drawing without an eraser."

John W. Gardner

Life is meant to be lived. We try to do it right, but sometimes we don't or we can't. Sometimes the distinction between what is right or wrong is not so apparent. We make choices. Should I play the piano or read a book? Take chemistry or biology? Volunteer at the homeless shelter or have a friend for dinner?

I like to think my life is kind of like a rich tapestry with a myriad of scenes. Some of the threads are interwoven between the scenes. The threads sometimes form rivers and streams to connect the scenes. My threads, my river and streams of life have been enriched by my love for Geda, my family, and my friends. Some of my challenges and experiences were like logs or dams that have caused my river to flow in ways that I could not have imagined. And yet, like the tapestry is a work of art, I hope my life is a beautiful work of art.

"Power is like being a lady...if you have to tell people you are, you aren't."

Margaret Thatcher

I liked that the powerful Margaret Thatcher is quoted for this statement. Admittedly, I am old-fashioned in some ways for my time. Manner, etiquette, politeness, articulate speech, a sense of decorum still impresses me. But humility - that essence of being real is at the core of what must be present.

Recently, I was at a board meeting where one person kept talking about all the important people he was friends with and another how she used to be a litigator (three times in the same meeting!). If you have to tell me how important you are, then in my book, you're not.

'Don't tell me, show me!'

"Music is the divine way to tell beautiful, poetic things to the heart."

Pablo Casals

Music can be so very powerful. I cannot recall a day that I have not heard music. In recent years, I am more aware though of music's power to energize and soothe and be expressive.

I think it is important to consider also that when we hum or sing it is a way to feel what is in our hearts. It can express emotions and feelings where words and silence fail.

Ronald Reagan said, "Life is one grand, sweet song, so start the music."

Enjoy, embrace the music of your life!

"Look up, laugh loud, talk big, keep the color in your cheek, and the buyer in your eye, adorn your person, maintain your health, your beauty and your animal spirit. "

William Hazlitt

Waking up early and going outside for a few minutes in the early sun has a powerful, uplifting effect on me. Sometimes, I need to jumpstart my day, push myself, get over myself, and get out of whatever blue Funk I'm in.

Think about what motivates you. What do you do for you? Sometimes, we can be so busy trying to please others that we neglect ourselves. It's okay, no, it's vital that you do what your inner spirit wants you to do. That's not to say it's easy, but if you are doing what you call yourself to do, you will be living your life to its fullest.

"If any of you cry at my funeral, I'll never speak to again."

Stan Laurel

Not that I will be able to speak to you. Hah! In the last couple of weeks, I've had too many people I know die or face the fact that they don't have long to live. But none of us knows when we will die.

Some people are always worrying - about their health, their job, their finances, or lack thereof. But worry robs one's day of joy.

Celebrate life!

Joan of Arc said, "One life is all we have and we live it as we believe in living it. But to sacrifice what you are and to live without belief is a fire more terrible than dying."

"Read every day, something no one else is reading. Think, every day, something no one else is thinking. Do, every day, something no one else would be silly enough to do. It is bad for the mind to continually be part of unanimity."

Christopher Morley

It's actually quite fun to try to read something that no one else is reading. Sometimes, I just try to find something interesting to be able to share.

Being purposefully silly is fun. I find that it makes me laugh at myself.

Discipline is good. Having good habits makes life simpler. But every once in a while, I think it's good to mix it up - have salad for breakfast, walk backward, write with my left hand, make funny faces, find something unusual, and take a photo.

"He who binds to himself a joy
Does the winged life destroy;
But he who kisses the joy as it flies
Lives in eternity's sunrise."

William Blake

As a child, I loved trying to catch lightning bugs at dusk on a warm summer night. And even though I tried to feed them with grass and weeds and give them air holes, by morning, they'd be gone. Reading this poem, I'm reminded that I loved the joy of being with my high school friends and later playing with my children, but life goes on.

Recognize the joys in life each moment of every day. See the birds, butterflies, trees and flowers, rain, snow and sunshine. Kiss the joy of being with people, the ones who bring us joy. But let them soar; let them be who they are meant to be!

"Sometimes our light goes out but is blown into flame by another human being. Each of us owes our deepest thanks to those who have rekindled this light."

Albert Schweitzer

I hope your light never goes out. But life gives us life. Sometimes, we experience grief or sadness or depression. There have been times when I have felt like I have nothing left in me to give, and I just wanted to curl up and cry. That's why it is important to keep connected with family and friends, to be honest about your feelings, and to listen to their feelings. It is in connecting with others that we are recharged, rekindled.

You may be the person to rekindle the light in someone else.

> *"There are two great days in a person's life - the day we are born and the day we discover why."*

> *William Barclay*

Sometimes, we know why we are born. There have been days that I have appreciated my unique gifts and realized that perhaps I was born to be in a certain moment and be the person who reached out to help another. But generally, I think life gives us life and we need to be continually aware of what we are supposed or going to do.

As a younger woman, I felt I was born to be a mother. At times, with my clients, I felt empowered that I was able to be there for them. Sometimes, I have felt that I was born to write, or sing or serve or be involved in my community. As I write this, perhaps I would describe 'why I was born' as to be 'in the moment,' to balance my work, family, community involvement, and give as much of myself as needed to make wherever I am better, and to make each person I meet in a day feel good.

"All we need to make us really happy is something to be excited about."

Charles Kingsley

My mother used to say we all need something to remember, something to do, and something to look forward to. It is about being excited about something. My older friends are great planners - parties, events to attend, and things they want to read or do.

To be enthusiastic about what you are doing brings so much joy and happiness. I can get excited making brownies for a get-together, thinking about who I will see, what I may learn and whose day I may brighten. The latter is what really makes me happy.

"My mission in life is not merely to survive; but to thrive; introduce so with some passion, some compassion, some humor and style. "

Maya Angelou

It's very powerful to state what we want in life. In business entities, the owners and boards spend a great deal of time crafting their mission statement. The mission statement of a well-run, successful company is a statement of purpose. Sure they, the owners and shareholders, may want to make money, but to be truly successful, a business must be committed to its purpose - whether it's providing a service or making a product.

A few years ago, Uncle Jeff gave me a five-minute journal. Each day challenged me to think about three things that were positive things I could do and to write out a statement or affirmation of who I envision myself to be. It's very powerful to spend time considering yourself as you want to be ...and then planning how to be you. Write your own mission statement!

"Before anything else, preparation is the key to success."

Alexander Graham Bell

Ah, yes? Preparation, the work. I used to marvel at people who could give speeches or athletes who made sports look easy or musicians who could entertain at a moment's notice. At some level, I knew they had practiced, but they made it look so easy.

Making it look easy is all about preparation. If you love what you are doing or you only want to accomplish something, the work that is the preparation becomes interesting. It can even become fun. "Fun." In high school, my Western Civilization teacher, Miss Hellman, would always say "we're going to have some fun today" before she gave us a pop quiz. I think it may have been fun for her, but I'm not sure we were of the same mind. But I digress.

Being passionate about and during preparation really is a joy in itself.

"The cure for anything is salt water: sweat, tears or the sea."

Isak Dineson

Recently, I learned that gargling with salt water is a good practice for good dental health. Perhaps salt water is not the cure for anything, but Isak Dineson is absolutely right about the power of sweat. Exercising or "working up a sweat" through our efforts not only cools the body but also gets rid of toxins. And tears, oh my yes. Crying for joy, tearing up at the sound of beautiful music, or seeing a child's delight as they excel in their effort is so very healing and cathartic. There is also a release of tension when I cry over my sadness or frustration.

And the sea. There are theories that the sea provides healing. For me, it is the walk and breathing of the air by the sea that emboldens and heals my soul.

May you truly embrace 'the salt of the earth'!

"As long as you live, keep learning how to live."

Lucius Annaeus Seneca

John Henry Newman said, "To grow is to change and to be perfect is to have changed often."

Each day of our lives is different. We must keep learning. Just because we graduate does not mean we stop learning. Learning new things, new processes, new ideas helps us adapt. It also helps us to engage with others.

If you think of recent history, people have learned to use computers and cell phones, have learned to stop smoking cigarettes, have learned about others, and hopefully have learned (or at least are learning) about the humanness of others and to live without discrimination and prejudice.

There is so much to learn. Learning to live well requires taking care of our bodies, our minds and our souls.

Life is short – keep learning to live it well!

"Better keep yourself clean and bright, you are the window through which you must see the world."

George Bernard Shaw

As I've gone through life, I have never wanted to experience the fog of vision impaired by drugs or alcohol. But it is not only substances that can blur or distort our vision of the world. We can be blinded by anger. Our view of the world can be bleak if we only allow negativity to surround us.

So, too can we have a misguided view of the world if we do not seek to learn and understand not only ourselves but our surroundings and the people in our lives.

Sometimes, it's easy to fall into bad habits. I can become a bit paranoid if I watch too many scary movies or even get depressed watching too many Hallmark movies where everyone seems to have a perfect life. Just like too much of anything… as the saying goes - 'we are what we consume'- we need to be aware of what we let into our minds too.

"Be faithful to that which exists within yourself."

Andre Gide

Learn about yourself. I mean, really learn. So often, I would have flitting ideas of what I could or might do. Explore those fleeting thoughts. You've already begun. When I was in my late thirty's, I was overweight and unfit. But I began to think that maybe I could train to do the first Cleveland Triathlon. I finished third in my age group (there were only 3); but I did it. It, the training and completion, taught me something about myself – my stubbornness, or tenacity, to get up and keep going when things were tough, that I could do something I previously thought was impossible, and that I like to write. Sharing my thoughts for an athletic journal helped me crystalize my core beliefs about the analogies of swim, bike, run to the balance I need in my life for family and friends, community and spiritual connection.

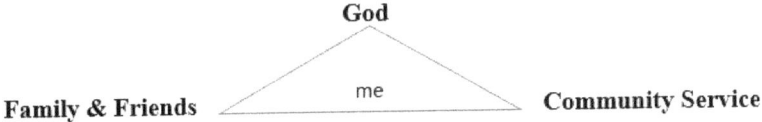

"We first make our habits, and then our habits make us."

John Dryden

Every once in a while, it is good to review what we do by habit. There are obvious ones like brushing our teeth or combing our hair that are good; biting one's nails or chewing with one's mouth open are not so good. Geda is a huge 'creature of habit' as they say. He's eaten peanut butter for breakfast for over fifteen years and he keeps a log of whether he's eaten enough greens and exercised enough each day.

Many years ago, I got into the habit of swearing. Not a very ladylike or courteous way to speak. And then I overused the word "like". Some habits a hard to break.

Habits, whether it is making my bed or reading fifteen minutes before I go to sleep, become so second nature that I might not be me without them.

> *"Be true to yourself.*
> *Help others,*
> *Make each day your masterpiece,*
> *Make friendship a fine art,*
> *Drink deeply from good books – especially the Bible,*
> *Build a shelter for a rainy day,*
> *Give thanks for your blessings, and*
> *Pray for guidance every day."*
>
> *John Wooden*

I'm always impressed with guests' answers on Scott Galloway's podcasts when he asks, "What advice would you give your younger self?" When I read this quote of John Wooden's, I thought, 'That's it!'

That is what I would tell my younger self. So, I share it with you.

"Lend yourself to others; but give yourself to yourself."

Michel Montagu

Don't give away all your stuff! I recently read if you put your hand over your heart and your other hand over your belly and close your eyes for 20 seconds and tell yourself you like yourself, it has an amazing positive effect.

Take care of you!

It sometimes feels to me that I get so busy helping others that I get exhausted. I am reminded by this quote to give myself some fun, some rest, some time to read.

Recognize what you need, and give it to yourself.

"Beginning today, treat everyone you meet is if they were going to be dead by midnight. Extend to them all the care, kindness and understanding you can muster, and do it with no thought of any reward. Your life will never be the same again."

Og Mandino

My Dad recognized that I had very little patience with people who were unkind to me or to others. I would want to tell them off or think of ways of making them feel bad, too. My Dad would say "don't lower yourself to their level." On my wedding day, one thing he said to me during our father-daughter dance was "never go to bed angry". Through the years, I've counseled many people and reminded myself to not leave things unsaid. If I remember that someone might not be alive tomorrow, it changes how I act today. It causes me to be less judgmental and to not regret my words or actions at the end of the day.

"We must let go of the life we have planned, so as to accept the one that is waiting for us."

Joseph Campbell

Your senior speech captured this concept of letting go so we can accept and are able to embrace what's ahead.

Plans and goals are wonderful. But as I often say, "life gives us life." Sometimes, we have challenges that make our plans or goals impossible. Oh, I can think of breaking my ankle and not being able to run long distances. But I also remember finding out two weeks before Uncle Jeff and Uncle Scott were born that instead of your Dad having one new sibling, he was going to have two.

I think we are called to evolve, to improve, to change for the better, and to be open to let go of how we thought it was going to be; and to live in the moment!

"There is no such thing as great talent without great will power."

Honore de Balzac

Very few human beings are born as geniuses or prodigies. Yet, even they must channel their gifts and have the willpower and fortitude to practice their talent.

Talent is like a muscle. When a person does not use it, the talent atrophies and disappears. I don't think I understood or appreciated willpower as a gift. Rather, I thought of it as a developed habit, but it is a mindset as well. Having the ability to be encouraged, to persevere, to stay motivated and to be determined is willpower. That is why I think it is important to recognize willpower as a gift, a talent to be used.

May you recognize your talents and have the willpower to share them as you like!

"We are what our thoughts have made us, so take care about what you think. Words are secondary. Thoughts live; they travel far."

Swami Vivekananda

I like the idea that our thoughts live; they travel far. Sometimes, I think I can hear the thoughts of family and friends who have died. That probably sounds creepy to you; I am sure a more logical explanation is my memory conjures up what they would say to me if they were alive. But, if my thoughts live, I hope they travel with you and let you know what a wonderful person you are and that I love you so very much.

"Nobody ever drowned in his own sweat."

Ann Landers

Okay, there's work to be done. I was 'blessed' as a young person to be instilled with what I call a strong work ethic. I was taught that if my Mom or Dad were working or cleaning, I was expected to help. And I was expected to not wait to be told what to do, but look for it.

Yet, I also think when our work makes us feel like we are drowning, it is time to reassess how we are spending our time. We are not slaves to our work or to anyone else. While hard work has tremendous benefits and rewards, I think it is extremely important to occasionally step back and evaluate whether I still appreciate the benefits and rewards of my work. Vacations are good, too!

"There is nothing in a caterpillar that tells you it's going to be a butterfly."

R. Buckminster Fuller

A good story usually has some element of surprise. It's true of interesting people as well. It's such a delight to watch a butterfly emerge from its cocoon. Perhaps it reminds me that the people I meet and I, as well, can evolve like the caterpillar and become the beautiful butterfly.

And since I was focused on observing nature… I am reminded of Franklin D. Roosevelt humorously observing —"I think we consider too much the good luck of the early bird and not enough of the early worm."

"To dare is to lose one's footing momentarily. Not to dare is to lose oneself."

Soren Kierkegard

Dare to dream big! Dare to think outside the box! Dare to try to do what you think might just be possible!

One can be daring in so many ways: trying for an advanced degree, substituting ingredients in a recipe, or joining a new group, to name a few. To be daring takes courage. Once you dare yourself to pursue your big dreams, you will be amazed at how enthusiastic and alive you will feel. In the process, you will gain confidence.

"Never let your sense of morals get in the way of doing what's right."

Isaac Asimov

Historically, we have witnessed and read about citizens who obeyed the law of reporting Jews being harbored by their neighbors.

I will provide a more personal recollection. In high school, a girl asked me to keep a secret. I felt that was my moral obligation and agreed. Her secret was that she feared she might be pregnant from having sex with her father. Doing what was right involved getting her help and revealing her secret. While I felt I had a moral duty to keep her secret, I felt she needed help more than my confidentiality. It was a very difficult decision.

Knowing what's right is not always easy. Doing what is right, what is honest, can take courage. Admitting our mistakes and failings though, allows us to maintain dignity and integrity.

"A little bit of mercy makes the world less cold and more just."

Pope Francis

Once in a while in life people have said or done unkind things. Sometimes, it may have been intentional. Sometimes, perhaps I deserved the unkindness. Other times, I realize now the unkindness was unintentional. Mercy embodies forgiveness and letting go of the hurt.

A wise priest shared with me that forgiveness is really something we give ourselves. The other person may not want our forgiveness or even feel they have done anything for which they should be sorry. I asked the priest, "but how can I forgive and forget?" He answered, "Again, forgiveness is a gift you give yourself. God gave you a brain so you don't forget."

People can make mistakes that hurt us. We can forgive them and show mercy.

"Appreciation is a wonderful thing; it makes what is excellent in others belong to us as well."

Voltaire

The excellence of an artist, or a bricklayer, or a car maker, or a dressmaker, or anyone who shares their talent makes our lives richer and more lovely. Yet, it is our appreciation that enriches our lives.

Saying thank you, smiling, clapping, hugging, high-fiving, and shaking hands may seem like you are giving, but in reality, when you show appreciation, it is really a gift to yourself. It is a recognition that you have experienced something special.

Being thankful and full of gratitude for my many blessings has become a habit for me. As I think about appreciation, though, I think it involves a bit of understanding and a recognition of the specialness of others.

"The most common way people give up their power is by thinking they don't have any."

Alice Walker

Stay informed! Speak up against injustices! I hate to break it to you, but there is evil in the world. While I believe most people may be capable of bad behavior, they are more than equally capable of good behavior. Sadly, I also think there are people who are just evil. Avoid them, but be aware of evil's existence. Know how to protect yourself physically and emotionally.

As human beings, we have the ability to speak, to draw, to write, to dance, to communicate with others through our expressions or touch. These gifts are very powerful. Be aware of your own unique, powerful gifts and use them wisely.

Also, I would be remiss if I did not tell of my strong belief in the power of prayer. I really mean its power. Certainly, I get that I have to 'work like I don't have a prayer and pray like I don't have any work.' Yet, I have seen miracles happen.

"Act the way you'd like to be and soon you'll be the way you act."

Leonard Cohen

Some girls want to be like their mothers and others don't want to be anything like their mothers. At the end of the day, I think we choose to emulate those we admire. As I meet with friends I have known all my life, I am fascinated with the way some of them have evolved. Some have embraced their interests to be educators, or financial advisors, or caregivers and others have stopped reading, become couch potatoes, or ceased being involved in their community.

On the negative side of acting mean, or wild, or snotty, it's pretty clear that one actually becomes how one acts.

I like to think if I act with calm and poise and dignity, that I will be calm, poised and dignified. Time will tell.

Choose how you want to act. What role do you want to play in life?

"The art of writing is the art of discovering what you believe."

Gustave Flaubert

Maybe it was my good teachers in grade school and high school who assigned topics for term papers that needed to explore a topic and then develop or argue a position that first taught me the truth of Flaubert's statement. Topics like 'the myth of racism' or 'the protestant ethic and the gospel of wealth' spurred me to research. But it was the writing process that really made me think, realize and discover what I believe.

Writing is an art. Whether it is sending a note to a friend, a letter to an editor of a newspaper, or writing a novel, art is expression. Writing is expression.

I don't know if I could write about what I do not believe. Frankly, I do not want to try. The discovery, research, learning and experience come first; then the joy of writing what I really think helps solidify and helps me discover what I truly believe.

"Sometimes it takes a good fall to really know where you stand."

Haley Williams

We all fall sometimes. We fail. We make mistakes. We don't meet others' expectations or our own. It's life. We are not perfect. Don't worry about it. In the end, we all die.

What is important is to dust ourselves off after we fall and figure out where we are. What we are going to do next because that is what we have – now.

We are all human, imperfect and real. We don't need to hide or flaunt our failures. But I think humility is being real about whom we are.

There is great power in knowing you have stood up and moved on from a fall or failure and have lived to tell about it.

"Morality is not the doctrine of how we may make ourselves happy, but how we make ourselves worthy of happiness."

Immanuel Kant

Are we not worthy of happiness? I disagree with Kant. My faith is that morality and worthiness have nothing to do with whether I am happy or not. Happiness is a choice!

My Mother would say 'you make your own fun!' If you go to a party, don't sit and wait for people to come to you. Get up and go meet them. We choose to see whether we are boring or interesting. We choose to be satisfied with what we have or be happy in the pursuit of having something more.

I won't give control to someone else to say 'you are worthy of being happy.' For me, morality comes down to treating others as I would like to be treated. But, as for making myself "worthy" of happiness – that choice is mine – and yours! Each of us is born worthy of happiness. Whether we are or not is our choice!

"It must be remembered that there is nothing more difficult to plan, more doubtful of success no more dangerous to manage than the creation of a new system. For the initiator has the enmity of all who profit by the preservation of the old institution and merely lukewarm defenders in those who would gain by the new one."

Nicolo Machiavelli

I've long said, 'change may be good, but transition sucks.' In the area of medicine, it sometimes seems as if finding cures for some diseases is fought against by big business. In law, it is the same. Even though the science showed the need for seat belts in cars, requiring them took years. As we now are thrust into a new realm of AI, it will be interesting to see how the old ways of thinking will be challenged.

Our more recent system of communicating using social media and texts reveals the challenges of managing a new system.

"Opportunities are like sunrises. If you wait too long, you miss them."

William Arthur Ward

Modern medicine is finding huge benefits to being exposed to experiencing early morning sun for ten minutes every morning. It's a gift we can give ourselves every morning. (At least most mornings given snow and rain.). But being aware of when the sun is first rising and being outside to feel that first light is pretty cool. The chance to observe what is around us is a great start to the day.

Seeing opportunities requires similar awareness. Academic, social, and career opportunities will come and go. The chance to visit someone or the time to call a friend or make someone else's day special may not be there in a month. Be aware of what opportunities you wish to pursue.

"People are like dirt. They can either nourish you and help you grow as a person or they can stunt your growth and make you wilt and die."

Plato

Choose with whom you wish to associate. As much as possible, surround yourself with people who, as Geda would say, 'are bigger, faster and stronger.' They'll make you be your better self.

Converse with and learn from intelligent people. One thing I've learned and continue to learn is that it is much more rewarding to have a conversation <u>with</u> people than <u>about</u> people.

I remember one of my favorite teachers shared a story of a friend of hers who loved to gossip. Mrs. Stearns related that the woman went to confession, and the priest told her for penance to take a feather pillow off the bed, cut it open and scatter the feathers out the window and then come see him the next week. When she returned, the priest told her to now go and gather the feathers. Impossible, just like not knowing how far gossip can spread.

"We know what we are, but know not what we may be."

William Shakespeare

We may know what we are. Sometimes, I think we can deceive ourselves and not really know what we are. Sometimes, we need another to offer constructive criticism. At times, I don't realize that I may be too judgmental or I don't realize how I may hurt another person's feelings. But generally speaking, I think we have a pretty good idea of what we are.

But considering what we may be is fascinating. At eighteen, I did not know I would be a wife, a mother, a grandmother, great aunt, etc. I had no idea of the people who would come into my life, the career choices I would make, or the myriad of experiences that have changed me and made me who I am today.

Humility is being real, knowing who you are. Faith is believing you can be a better self.

"Look up at the stars, not down at your feet. Try to make sense of what you see, and wonder what makes the universe exist. Be curious."

Stephen Hawking

Never stop asking questions and searching for answers. I find that I think I know something and then have to verify if my knowledge is accurate. Sometimes, I still find I need to look up words and their meanings. Reading about foreign affairs, I need to relearn the location of certain countries. Trying to figure out new technology, how things are made or even how to make a new recipe adds such enrichment. Being curious about others and asking them questions helps me connect with them.

Not everything you read or hear is accurate. Ask questions and don't be gullible to think someone else is always correct!

"Who would set a limit to the mind of man?

Who would assert that we know all there is to be known?"

Galieo Galdei

The history of civilization is so filled with inventions and breakthroughs of understanding. The possibilities of what we may yet learn are endless.

The human brain and inner workings of the human body are miraculous. And we are still learning how the body and the brain work together.

Imagine what we may learn from trees that have been around for hundreds of years, from creatures in the sea, or from our solar system and beyond.

I hope your passion for learning is ever present all of your life. There are no limits to what we may learn!

"Persevere with a plan to reach your passion, and life will be good."

Homer Hickman

Jim Rohn said, "If you don't design your own life plan, chances are you'll fall into someone else's plan. And guess what they have planned for you? Not much."

You may have a plan for the next 50 years or maybe just a plan for the afternoon. If you can, and you can spend some time thinking about your goals. Think about what your gut tells you that you should do. Meditate or pray about what you think you want to do. Then plan; set your action plan.

Life will give you life, and Plan A may dovetail with Plan B, or C, or D, but just as a clock helps us keep track of time, if you persevere with your plan for that which you love, the rewards are tremendous.

"Take your role seriously, but do not take yourself seriously."

Stephen A. Malbasa - Geda

No doubt you will have serious roles in your life. It's important to be the best you can be in those roles. With your job(s), with your relationships, with your community involvement be serious. As Fred Rogers said, "Play is really the work of children; play is serious learning." – What I am trying to convey is play. Have fun. Continue to be child-like all your life. We don't have to be serious to do a good job.

But the role is the role; it is not all about you.

You may deserve the role; you may have fame and fortune but do not be conceited.

Be awesome, humble and kind!

"We have a finite amount of time. Whether short or long, it doesn't matter. Life is to be lived."

Randy Pausch

The Last Lecture, by Randy Pausch would be one of my most recommended reads. So many words of wisdom!

None of us knows how long we may live. Live!

Dare to dream big! Work hard to make your dreams a reality.

Consider how you are spending your time. Connect with people! People are more important than things or money. Make them happy to be around you. Try to make someone else's day better because of you and what you do.

And from me, Madie, I think I want to share the song and poem of my early childhood.

Louisa May Alcott – from my memory – may not be exact.

"Little drops of water,
Little grains of sand,
Make the mighty waters,
And the pleasant lands.

Thus the little moments,
Humble though they be,
Make the mighty ages
Of eternity."

Each and every moment is precious. May you have joy in each and every moment and laughter often.

And being a moon child and affected by the wondrous cycles of the moon…

By Clifton Johnson

"I see the moon, and the moon sees me.
The moon sees somebody I'd like to see.
So, God bless the moon;
And God bless the somebody I'd like to see.
If I get to heaven and you're not there,
I'll write your name on the golden stair.
I'll write it big so the angels can see
Just how much you mean to me."

You mean so very much to me, Madie!

Love,

Baba